MAD-LY YOURS!

by Sergio Aragones

Edited by Albert B. Feldstein

PAPERBACK LIBRARY

NEW YORK

PAPERBACK LIBRARY EDITION
First Printing: June, 1972

This Paperback Library Edition is published by arrangement
with E. C. Publications, Inc.

Paperback Library is a division of Coronet Communications, Inc. Its
trademark, consisting of the words "Paperback Library" accompanied by
an open book, is registered in the United States Patent Office. *Coronet
Communications, Inc., 315 Park Avenue South, New York, N.Y. 10010.*

To Jerry De Fuccio

THE SUPERCHARGED SWORDSMAN

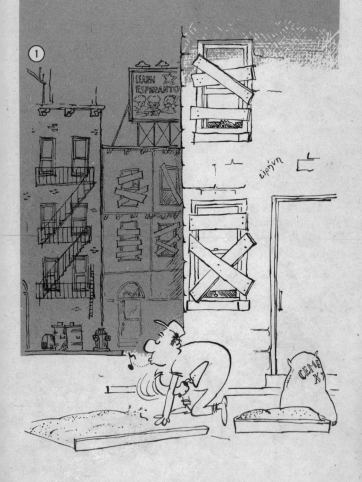

PITFALL IN AFRICA

BIBLE BELT

CANINE CUNNING

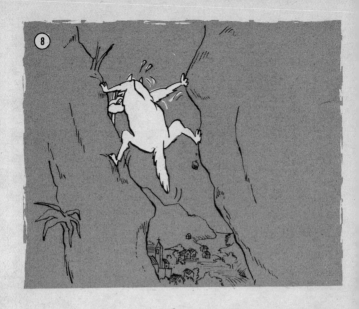

WITHIN THE LAW

THE NEXT HEAVYWEIGHT CHAMPION

①

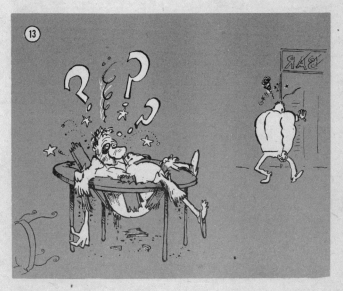

SOME GOOD ADVICE!

GOING INTO ANOTHER RACKET

THE CIVIC-MINDED TURN OUT

①

THE GREAT ESCAPE

THE BEAST IN THE BARGAIN BASEMENT

ON A PROMINENT MIDTOWN LEDGE

AWAITING A VACANCY

THE SOCIAL LION

HIS CUP RUNNETH UNDER

THE FATEFUL HOUR

①

APPEASEMENT ON MAIN STREET

CAUGHT IN A SPIN

①

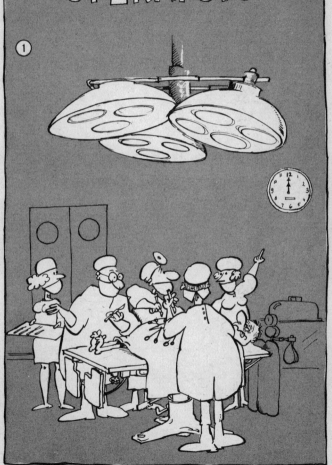

A LONGHAIR CONCERTO

POSING A PROBLEM

THE PHOTO-FINISH

ONE FOR THE BOOKS

A WEIGHTY DECISION

SOUTH AMERICAN
BRAINSTORM

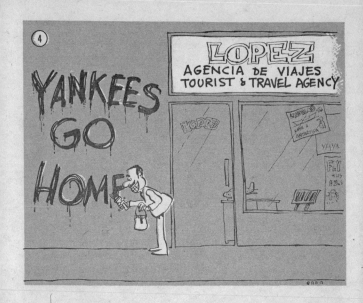

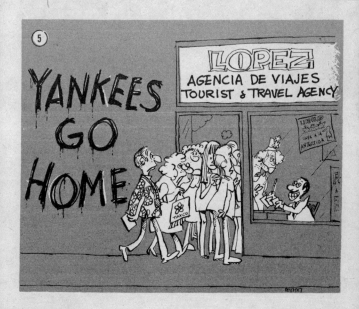

PREPARE FOR DESCENT

POINT OF VIEW

①

THE STILL LIFE PAINTER

THE RINK
OF
DISASTER

CONCRETE
EVIDENCE

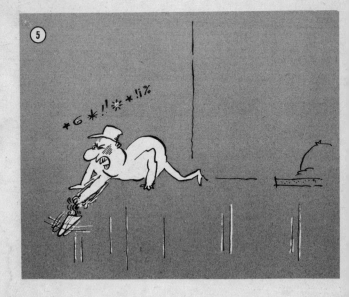

ON-THE-JOB TRAINING

GLORIES OF THE REVOLUTION

WHILE VISITING THE CITY DUMP

ONE SLOW NIGHT IN YUCATAN

JUNGLE BUNGLE

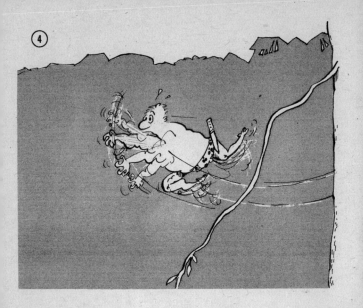

MAD-LY
YOURS!
ARAGONÉS